Geisha: Japanese, from gie (art) and sha (person).

Sales Geisha is the art of sales.

Christine Miller

Create Space Publishing
Scotts Valley, CA

Sales Geisha

ISBN:1523882360
ISBN-13:9781523882366

DEDICATION

To my family, and to all those that wish to excel in sales.
The salesperson in me salutes the salesperson in you.

Contents

Sales Philosophy

Sales Tips

Customer Service

Recruitment and Retention

Sales Compensation

Sales Geisha

Sales: an exchange of goods or property for money
Geisha: Japanese, from *gie* (art) + *sha (*person or doer)

*A collection of essays for the person
desiring to manage the art of sales.*

Sales Geisha

Introduction
Why Sales Geisha?

In 1997, *Memoirs of a Geisha*, by Arthur Golden, was published. The story of Sayuri became an international bestseller and I too was captivated by the tale.

Sayuri's life was one filled with hardship. Geishas were depicted as girls that had their virginity auctioned to the highest bidder, followed by an adult life entertaining men. At its harshest and most incorrect depiction, geishas are seen as prostitutes.

Why is it then that I have come to name my book *Sales Geisha*? It would seem that such a title would represent sales people and particularly sales women as agents who manipulate their customers and use sex to close deals. In that regard a Sales Geisha would be a bad salesperson, and also a type of sales prostitute.

That is not the Sales Geisha story that I want to tell.

It's been a number of years since I first read the novel, and I have been unable to shake how a true geisha, and her training, can be translated to success in the world of sales. I read of how an onee-san (mentor) trained the maiko (apprentice geisha).

An onee-san is the most important person to a young maiko. She is a big sister of sorts, taking her to see clients while the young geisha observes. The onee-san teaches the maiko everything she needs to be successful: how to pour tea, the proper language to use, and how to conduct herself with customers. When an error is made the onee-san corrects the maiko. The young geisha learns everything from her trainer, the onee-san. Sounds like the best onboarding to me.

In fact, the young geisha even takes on a name that is a derivative of her mentor. The onee-san has so much trust in her trainee, that she gives her part of her name. The mentor essentially declares to clients that she has trained this geisha and has trust in her skills. The new geisha is also not allowed to have her own clients until she can prove she has learned all her skills, and passed all her tests.

Would you stake your reputation on your sales team? Give them your name? Do your sales people work with clients before they are skilled and knowledgeable in their trade?

Geishas are highly respected in Japan, and geisha means "artist". They are more than just beautiful dancers, and true geishas are not prostitutes. They are often misunderstood by those outside of the Japanese culture. I often feel that sales is often misunderstood in the same way. Being successful in sales is more than fancy lunches and incentives. And, we are not the prostitutes of the company.

Just as the geisha is disciplined to learn the skills of her trade, a good sales agent will also be disciplined to learn her trade. The poor imitations are the ones that cause the world to think less of geishas and salespeople.

This somewhat abstract connection between geisha and sales has made me a better salesperson and trainer. I only hire people that I feel will represent my name well, and I train them to be great.

Behind the painted smiles of the geisha and the confidence of a salesperson is a professional that makes sure every customer is satisfied. These professionals use wit, skill and intelligence to become successful.

Use the model of the Sales Geisha to improve your team. And, the next time you meet a great salesperson show your appreciation. This individual possesses talents and abilities that are extraordinary.

Sales Geisha

Sales Geisha

Part 1

Sales Philosophy

Easy Steps to Tell Your Story

Many years ago, I was working in retail, when my store manager pointed to a sale end-cap and asked me, "What story are you telling with this display?" He went on to describe how every display should tell the customer a story, and those stories should match the overall message of the company.

Integrate these tips into your daily routine, and share your business story with everyone you touch!

Be authentic.
What is your personal story? Is your company laid back and relaxed, or high energy and intense? Are you family-friendly or do you target white-collar professionals? If you are unsure, you can analyze your own style and match your company's story to your personal style. This authenticity will trickle down to your employees and to your customers. Successful companies have leaders that motivate through their personal style. Think Steve Jobs, (innovative and detail oriented) and Sam Walton, (value and customer focused). Two very different styles, but both authentic and easy to translate to employees and customers. People will follow you when you are true to yourself.

Hire authentic people.
Notice I didn't say, "hire people like you." You need different types of people with diverse backgrounds and ideas, not drones that think and act exactly the way you do. The key is to find people who can be passionate about what you are hiring them to do *and* buy into the story you want to tell. For example, let's imagine you have a silly creative, work atmosphere. Your accountant will need to be passionate about accounting, as well as support and be excited, about the idea that your business environment is fun, not stodgy.

Pay attention to the details.
Remember my store manager's wisdom? Every part of the store (and your business) has to tell your story. That's right, it's time to bring the creative team, the sales people, the line workers and the finance folks all on the same page. And, yes, I realize in some instances all of those people are just you! Your website, your offices, your store and your

marketing all need to "say" the same thing. Is your website style "fun," but your employees walk around in ties and frowns on their faces? Does your restaurant target families, but lack a baby changing station? Pay attention to the details, they matter!

Be the End User.
Take one hour every month and become a target customer of your business. Sometimes we become so busy, we forget to look at our business from our customers' perspective. Do you have a beautiful, creative display behind a dirty window? Are your employees smiling? Is your online store easy to find and use? Walk around the office and through the sales floor. Check out the bathrooms and the warehouse. Spend some time on your website. Buy your product from your employees. Find out the story that is being told and make sure it's the one you want!

What Jurassic Park Taught Me About Sales and Marketing

In 1993, the first Jurassic Park packed theaters and broke sales records. Most people left the movie in awe of the special effects and unique story line. I recently re-watched the movie and was reminded of what resonated most with me, the first time I saw the film. It was the clear and impactful sales and marketing message. Yes, I walked away from Jurassic Park with a lesson in sales and marketing. More specifically, I learned from the velociraptors, commonly known as raptors.

Remember the raptors? They hunted in packs and were contained behind an electrified fence. Not wanting to stay penned in, every day they systematically tested the system for weaknesses. They also remembered where they attacked and would never attack the same place twice. I watched that scene and thought, that's how remarkable sales and marketing people work.

Tenacity and Strategy

Think about it. How many times do marketers approach a client with the same offer, same pitch, only to be told no, over and over again? The velociraptors didn't test the same place twice, and they didn't give up. They continually looked for a weakness in the electrical system. A weakness in the fence was an opportunity for the raptors to escape the pen and get into the park.

In marketing we look for growth opportunities, a way "in" to reach our customers. The raptors were tenacious and had a thoughtful strategy. Do you? Train yourself to think before you get burned, and don't continue to make the same mistake. Remember how you failed and re-approach with a new angle. Learn from your mistakes. Be tenacious. Think.

Teamwork and a Creative Offense

In Jurassic Park the raptors were the last of the predators to endure. Every other dinosaur in the film could be avoided or defeated. The raptors attacked with preparation that was different from the others. They worked as a team and approached from the side instead of head-on. They had a plan that that was rehearsed and executed precisely. In Jurassic Park, the weak did not survive. The same can be said for many business segments. Is your sales and marketing team built to endure? Are they easily defeated?

Be mindful of your sales and marketing method, and be known for a unique and creative style. The raptors knew they would be expected from the front, and unexpected from the side. Anticipate the barriers in your path, and tackle them in a surprising way. Know the obstacles and objections you will face, and be prepared to overcome them before they are used as a defense. Break out of the pen and be different. Be the last to survive.

Marketing and Sales People as Vicious Dinosaurs?

Now I'm not saying that marketing and salespeople are like small vicious dinosaurs (although I have encountered a few), but rather we could learn from the strategy displayed in the film. How can your company evolve beyond the competition? Strategize like the raptors; never attack the same place twice. Approach the challenge from different angles, and present solutions you haven't offered, benefits you have not explained.

In Jurassic Park, the strategy of the raptors worked, and they escaped. The strategy of the raptors can work for you too.

Become a Sales Cowboy!

The Wild West...such an awesome period in history. Six gun shooters, lawlessness, fighting off attacks, cowboys saving the day. No formal codes were in place, but pioneers were bound by the unwritten rules of good deeds, fairness, and respect for the land. It made me wonder, is it time to become a sales cowboy?

Ramon Adams, author of the 1969 book, *The Cowman and His Code of Ethics,* states: "Back in the days when the cowman with his herds made a new frontier, there was no law on the range. Lack of written law made it necessary for him to frame some of his own, thus developing a rule of behavior that became known as the "Code of the West." In sales we often have structure, but no formal rules for behavior, or "laws on the range". Plans, goals, objectives, CRM's, and metrics all make selling more successful and efficient. But what if we took the best sales practices and combined them with the Code of the West? Could we become even more successful? After all, aren't we blazing new frontiers with every new client call while we strive to expand our territory? Should we all strive to be sales cowboys?

**"A man's got to have a code, a creed
to live by, no matter his job."
John Wayne**

Code of the West	Code of Sales Cowboy
Remove your guns before sitting at the dining table.	Leave your emotions at the door. This is business, not a reality TV show.
Don't make a threat without expecting dire consequences.	Nothing to change- Don't make a threat without expecting dire consequences. It happens.

Code of the West	Code of Sales Cowboy
Never pass anyone on the trail without saying "Howdy".	Be respectful, friendly and gracious to everyone, including gatekeepers and receptionists.
Always fill your whiskey glass to the brim.	Be careful if you fill your whiskey glass to the brim. Not everyone is Don Draper, and he hit the wall a few times.
A cowboy doesn't talk much.	Talk less, listen more.
No matter how weary and hungry you are after a long day in the saddle, always tend to your horse's needs before your own.	Yes, your client is your horse. Take care of them first and foremost, and they will take care of you.
Do not practice ingratitude. A cowboy is pleasant even when out of sorts. Complaining is what quitters do, and cowboys aren't quitters.	Say thank-you all the time, and every time. A good salesperson is pleasant even when out of sorts. Clients don't care about our complaints, nor should they have to hear about them.

Code of the West	Code of Sales Cowboy
Always be courageous. Cowboys don't tolerate cowards.	Go for the big appointment, presentation or sale. You don't fail when trying; you fail when you don't even try.
A cowboy always helps those in need, including strangers and enemies.	Be a good person and good things will come your way. Yes, I believe in Karma.
Give your enemy a fighting chance.	Play fair. Cheating is for losers. The win is so much better when it comes legitimately.
Cowboys are modest.	If your ego is so big, you have trouble fitting your head through the door, you won't be invited to the table (and you might end up in a painful situation trying to jam your way in!)
A cowboy is loyal to his "brand," to his friends, and those he rides with.	Don't sell something you don't believe in and don't poach from your co-workers, they are your posse.

Code of the West	Code of Sales Cowboy
Honesty is absolute - your word is your bond, a handshake is more binding than a contract.	Shake hands and mean it. Make your word stronger and more binding than a contract.
Live by the Golden Rule.	Treat others as you should be treated: with tolerance, consideration, and compassion.

Sales and Marketing Can Work Together

Remember the Reese's Peanut Butter commercials from the '80's? Two strangers are walking, one eating a chocolate bar, the other spooning out peanut butter. Engrossed in their snacks they collide. One person exclaims, "You got your peanut butter in my chocolate!" and the other exclaims, "You got your chocolate in my peanut butter!" They sample the mixture and we hear the slogan "Two great tastes that taste great together." Sales and marketing are "two great departments that should work together".

The Dynamics

In small businesses, the marketing and sales tasks are often done by the same department, or by one person. In larger corporations, these two teams are more distinctive, with different goals and often at odds. The marketing side thinks that salespeople don't know how to take advantage of the advertising, spend too much time focusing on individual accounts, and can't see the big picture. The sales team thinks the marketing side spends too much money on research and advertising and not enough on sales incentives and improving relationships. Should one group tackle both tasks? Or should these two teams work together? With such differences, and so much at stake, it would seem that a fast and furious "No!" would be the correct answer to both questions.

Integration

Sales and marketing are often separate divisions within an organization, and when they do work together, they don't always get along. Should they? Sales and marketing teams do have something in common, the buyer. Marketing studies the buyer and determines the advertising medium and message. Salespeople have one-on-one interactions with the buyer. The buyer provides revenue, and increased revenue is the foundation of business growth.   Sales and marketing are like chocolate and peanut butter. Different, yet surprisingly delicious when properly blended together.

"Everybody" is Not a Target

I always flinch a little if I'm in a meeting and hear that "everyone" is the target or customer of a product or service. Everyone? Really? The mindset behind this belief is that "anybody" may need the product, so why eliminate any potential customers? This theory has business owners believing that segmenting your market can result in lost revenue. Isn't it better to have some money in the coffers than none at all?

Once upon a time in America, big businesses were able to market to mass audiences. Unfortunately (or fortunately), that era ended along with three martini lunches. Mass marketing techniques that worked in the 20th century are not the way to market in the 21st century. Marketing today favors uniqueness. The truth is that you will accept business from anyone, but shouldn't try to sell to everyone. McDonald's, with an advertising budget that exceeds 2 billion, does not mass market. They target children, youth and young urban families. So if McDonald's, with a 2 billion budget, segments its sales outreach, shouldn't you?

Everybody is not a target. Back to the question of filling the coffers….what about ROI? Return on Investment. People invest in marketing and sales to make a higher return. If you have to invest a significant amount of time, money and energy to acquire a low level client, is it a good investment? If you have a positive return on investment, but it could have been a higher return, you have still wasted money. Unfortunately most of those low level clients equate to high investment, low return when it comes to sales. If you are selling a ground pork patty, (shaped to vaguely resemble a mini rack of ribs), covered in barbecue sauce and onions, and pickles on a roll, for $3, should you market it to someone who is looking for a five-star dining experience?

Seth Godin, entrepreneur and marketer, speaks of Otaku in his Ted Talk, *"How to get Ideas to Spread"*. What is Otaku? It's a Japanese term for people that are obsessed with a product. People with Otaku for your product will buy and help spread the word. McDonald's knows this. Their McRib sandwich has such a strong following that there are websites that log McRib "sightings". (I'm not kidding, Google it and you can see if the McRib is available near you!) These customers are so passionate about their McRib that they are willing to drive, sometimes hundreds of miles, to buy the product. These people are obsessed for sure.

There's a great quote by Brian Chesky of Airbnb where he says: *"It's better to build something that 100 people love than 1 million kind of like."* Great advice. Focus your time and energy on cultivating those clients with Otaku for your product or service. Not only will they produce the most revenue for your company, they will be your best salespeople. They will offer endorsements and referrals, as well as share positive stories to their colleagues and on their social networks. They will also provide you with valuable, honest feedback about problems and improvements, thus paving the way for an improved product and greater sales.

Identify who has Otaku, who does want what you are selling, and then sell, sell, sell! You can't please everyone, so don't try to. You do need customers, we all do, and I understand. However, sometimes the secret to success is knowing what not to do, and who *not* to target! As hard as it is to write, and maybe for you to accept, not everyone is your customer.

Sales Geisha

.

Sales Geisha

Part 2

Sales Tips

Networking for Business Development

We've all heard about the power of networking. "It's not what you know but who you know" is a phrase that often is repeated in business discussions. Yet many networking experiences leave a negative impression. Maybe at your last mixer you were nervous about meeting someone new, didn't know what to say, or you were ignored. Your biggest worry was the fear of coming off as too pushy.

To overcome these obstacles and produce meaningful results you will need to make a commitment of time, energy and resources. With proper planning you will be able to acquire new clients, cross-sell other opportunities and maintain existing clients through expanded business relationships. A networking action plan will get you on your way.

Create Goals

Define your networking goals. What do you hope to achieve? Do you want to meet people or a specific person? Do you want to build your reputation or generate referrals? Answer these questions honestly and specifically. With measurable results you'll be able to measure the success of your goals.

Develop a Plan

Determine the best events to attend and organizations to join. Ask existing customers which events they attend and what they liked about those events. If you want to expand your connections in new energy technologies, join an organization whose focus is on green business. Interested in entrepreneurs? Join a networking group that supports those people. In every community there is a variety of organizations. Invest time and research matching your goals with events. Determine how many events you want to attend in a month and then plan on attending slightly more than that number. If you miss one, you're not behind.

Be Prepared

Have a memorable introduction prepared. This is often known as your "elevator pitch". Your introduction should include who you are and what you do. Include information that is relevant to the person you are meeting and talk about benefits, not features of your work. Here's an example of a bad elevator pitch. "Hi, I'm Joe Jones of Acme Corporation based in Burlington, Vermont. We are a human resources company specializing in career management for business professionals." Now this is a legitimate description of a company. As an elevator pitch, it stinks. Sounds boring, doesn't it? Now here is a much better example for the same company. "Hi, I'm Joe Jones of Acme Corporation, the state's leading publisher of books, audio programs and seminars for business professionals on how to manage their careers. We don't help these folks with their business; we educate them on how to get jobs, get promoted and become successful." This introduction is also a description, but it's a description of the benefits, not the features of the company. It's also interesting and opens the door to questions and continuing the conversation. Plan and practice your introduction. It should only be about 20 to 30 seconds long. Behavioral studies show that it only takes about five seconds for a person to make up their mind whether or not they like you, and only an additional 10 to 15 seconds to determine if he/she will buy something from you.

Bring Your Best Game.

Get the most out of networking events by interacting with integrity. Be helpful and positive. Have you ever been stuck chatting with a person who laments over the state of the economy, bad weather all that is negative? Don't be that person! Share your ideas and be helpful. Connect colleagues together when you can. Know a good accountant and someone who is looking for one? Make the introduction. The favor will be returned to you sometime. Respect confidentiality and listen to your new contact. Don't scan the room looking to see if someone more important or better is available to meet.

Attend mixers, expos, and conferences with confidence. You can't guarantee some one else's success, but if working with you makes them achieve their goals faster, better, and more efficiently, you'll be a part of their winning team. Now you just have to pitch it.

Social Selling

Social selling; it's not asking about your client's weekend or their kids. It's about utilizing social media to increase sales. Do you know how it works and should your sales reps even care?

Sales has always been about doing business with people you know. Networking and leveraging relationships through meetings, conferences, organizations, etc., has been the traditional path to create connections. The advent of social media has changed this model. Gone are the days of sitting at your desk "working the phones." Social selling is the use of social media for generating leads and advancing sales. It is based on relationship building; with customers knowing whom you are before you engage them in the sales cycle.

With Sales 2.0 technology, customers can obtain company and product data long before they meet with you. Considering the majority of prospects never (or almost never) take a meeting from a cold call or e-mail, progressive salespeople need to know how to go from click to closed.

To begin social selling, you need to understand it. Social selling leverages social media in order for you to identify with your customers and their influences. Traditional techniques are time consuming and limit the exposure a rep can achieve with their client base. Social selling enables salespeople to expand their reach exponentially simply by using technology that allows them to socialize on a grander scale.

Easy Steps to Social Selling
1. Find out where your customers "hang out" on-line.
   Be present in places that are relevant to them, not you! Visit their cyber haunts (Facebook, Twitter, Linked In, You Tube, Pinterest, etc.) and read their posts and comments.

2. Sign up on their sites and add their social profiles to your customer relation management (CRM) tools. Signing up is like asking for someone's business card. It will allow you to become more aware of that person's needs, wants and interests, and you'll be able to learn more from that content than you can from some face-to-face meetings!

3. Follow blogs. Set an RSS feed on your client's blogs and on their industry blogs. They may give you give the best information about your customers or their industry.

4. Listen, listen and listen!
   One of the toughest tasks for a salesperson s to know when to be quiet and let the customer have the floor. Those silent times allow the client to think and speak, and share info that we desperately seek. The same principle applies to social selling. Don't immediately jump on a site and start your sales pitch. Listen to find out what your customer is saying about themselves, their company, their problems and competition.

5. Gather information by creating Google Alerts for customers and their competitors. Prospects and customers will voluntarily, and publicly, scatter sales clues if you listen actively.

6. Finally, reach out and make contact. Leave a message on a wall or share a tweet. Introduce your customer to other professionals that can be an asset, or share a great link. Respond to a blog. When you see that they have a problem you can help with, reach out. Make yourself available in any medium where they are comfortable; on-line, on the phone, or in person.

With Social Sales, intelligence is key. Social media is changing the way people shop, and your salespeople need to know how to engage them. This is the new reality of sales.

Sales vs. Order Taking

Are your best producers sales people or order takers? Which one do you need and can you tell the difference? Would you call the person at the coffee shop a sales person or an order taker? They manage a business exchange between customers and the store (sales), and yet they primarily take orders. Is the clerk who upsells a sales person, or still an order taker? This type of sales confusion can make it difficult to seek and hire the appropriate sales professional. It's often challenging for an employer to differentiate the roles, and also challenging for reps to properly label themselves. Know what you need, (and what you're getting), before you hire.

Order Taker
The order taker waits for contact from the buyer and the buyer dictates the sale. They respond to RFP's and react to requests. The order taker is controlled by the customer, and sells in the now. He is adept at describing product features and how the purchase can benefit the buyer. They are advocates for the customer and what the customer demands. The order taker doesn't actually have to sell; instead they survive on "low hanging fruit." Their goal is to close the deal and move on to the next call. Marketing a well-known brand in a healthy economy can result in a large income for the order taker.

Salesperson
A salesperson hunts for prospects. He is focused on his customer's needs and develops a relationship. The customer is engaged in the sales process and the rep influences the buy. A salesperson has a sales strategy, often selling 6 -12 months in advance. He plans for the future of the customer and the company, looking beyond the here and now. Low-hanging fruit is not perceived as the main course, but rather sales "gravy". It's appreciated as an easy win, not a sustainable way to make goal. The salesperson is constantly prospecting, and a top performer will earn a large income in any economy.

Know the difference between an order taker and an order maker. Determine the type of calls and leads you are receiving before you decide on which type of professional to hire. Many order takers pose as sales people, so make sure you have a thorough vetting process. A good salesperson can change the course of your business while an order taker chooses the path of least resistance. There is a place and a role for both professions in the sales field, but hiring the wrong talent can prove disappointing and costly.

Sell Like You're on QVC

As a career salesperson, I love dealing with good salespeople and watching the process. With that said, I am fascinated with QVC. Launched in 1986, the Westchester, PA channel broadcasts live, 24-hours a day, seven days a week (except Christmas). They offer approximately 600,000 products annually and average 15,000 orders an hour. QVC (stands for Quality, Value, Convenience) is a 7.5 billion-a-year company and has a sales rate of $6,000 a minute! Now that's some sales numbers that get my attention.

Most people tune into QVC and watch, credit card in hand, ready to jump on the phone or log onto the site to make a purchase. I, on the other hand, love watching the selling. The hosts of the show engage every sales tool to transform casual watchers to impulsive buyers.

Here's how they do it (and you can do it too!):

Ability to Describe the Product Quickly and Succinctly. A QVC product is given 6 to 7 minutes of airtime. In order to generate sales, you need to be able to describe your product quickly and effectively. Imagine you were given the opportunity to present your business to thousands of potential customers in a very short time. What would you do? Practice, practice, practice! Pretend every sales opportunity is a QVC show. Know your product, and look polished. Whether on QVC or face-to-face, rambling is a waste of time, and wasted time is a wasted sales opportunity.

Features vs. Benefits. On QVC you will learn about every detail of a product, but you'll also learn how you can benefit from those features. In fact, little did you know how much easier, cleaner, happier, stylish, thinner, etc.; you'd be, if only you had this "thing".

Testimonials- I love hearing from Annabelle in Georgia who has bought and loved the product. She can personally share how the item has changed her life. What a clever way to work in product endorsements. If she can afford it, use it and love it, so can we!

Frequency- As consumers we may be interested in a product, but need constant prodding in order to take action. In the marketing world we call that frequency. The higher the frequency message, the more likely we are to buy. QVC repeats their advertising message over and over again, in a short amount of time. They have a higher ad frequency rate in one product broadcast than most full fledge ad campaigns.

Call to Action- Every good ad needs a call to action. QVC creates a sense of urgency and call to action by having limited time offers and showing you that they are running low on a product. Call now or you may not get the color, style, or amount that you want.

Pricing- Take something that's a little large in one sum and break it down into EZ payments. Suddenly that $120 purchase seems affordable at only $20 a month. Don't highlight the full purchase price, highlight the low monthly payment. (Also include a call to action saying that EZ pay won't be available next time you see the product for sale!)

Create Repeat Customers- It's much easier to generate revenue from existing customers than create new ones, right? QVC knows this and packages many of its products on auto-delivery. At the initial sale they sell you more! They create a long-term customer at the first sale.

Look at your sales process. Do you incorporate all the above tactics when selling a customer? How can you sell more like QVC? Watch it and learn. Try not to buy something. I dare you!

Sales Geisha

Sales Geisha

Part 3

Customer Service

Etiquette Mistakes:
How Bad Manners Cost Business Owners

Manners. *Definition: The socially correct way of acting; etiquette.* I've been thinking a lot about manners lately and have begun to wonder. When has it become acceptable to be rude? At some point we all have had a door slammed in our face, or sat next to someone yelling into a cell phone at a restaurant. In many ways it's like Mr./Ms. Rude are oblivious to others in their environment. Unfortunately this egocentric sloppiness has also transcended to business practices.

Let's start at the beginning. You are considering buying a product or hiring a service provider. You contact possible contractors, set up an appointment and request a proposal. You decide not to move forward with the product, not to work with a particular company, or the budget deems the purchase out of reach. Please contact the vendors involved and tell them about your decision. Salespeople are very accustomed to hearing no and to understanding budget constraints. Sharing your decision is a fair request and a quick exit meeting is more time effective than dodging follow up calls and e-mails.

Next, don't dodge or ignore follow up calls and e-mails. Yes, you are busy. Everyone is busy. Yet people always have time for the things that are important to them. A quick follow up with a better time to talk, or a no, is still better than leaving a potential business vendor or customer out in the void. Don't be oblivious to others in your environment.

Say thank you. Say thank you for the meeting, the proposal, the time, the follow-up and the effort. This should happen no matter how the business meeting ends. People do business with people they know and trust. Become a business that people trust and want to work with, even if that isn't today.

Why the formality, when ignoring someone is the universal sign for "I'm too busy" or "The answer is no"? Because this is your business and your business reputation is largely based on your behavior. And because

people share, even salespeople and vendors. They share in their recommendations, their perceptions and their experiences. And now they share via worldwide free platforms like Twitter, Facebook, and Yelp. And they talk at chamber mixers and over coffee with friends. Do you want to be categorized as someone with a good product with poor follow through? A business that is difficult to work with? Someone who expects exceptional accommodations with quick proposals and then disappears? Maybe you've never thought about it, or thought it important. Well, think about it now, because a negative impression can cost your business. Everybody shares. And most people don't follow the dictate "If you can't say something nice…."

How You Lose Clients Who Love You (And It's Not For the Reasons You Think)

Your product is great, pricing competitive, and employees are likeable. Yet you can't seem to take the business to the next level and grow. Attrition is high, why don't clients that initially love you, stay with you?

You own your business because you have a unique talent, service or idea. However that doesn't mean you are a great accountant, receptionist, bookkeeper, HR director and marketer. As a small business owner it is crucial to know your strengths and accept your weaknesses. Customers demand good service from the estimate to the final bill. As a business owner it's easy to believe you can do it all. Trying to wear too many hats can lead to mistakes and oversights. Studies show business-service clients can be up to five times more likely to switch professionals for perceived service quality problems than for price concerns or product quality issues. Interesting, huh? You are losing clients because of poor service and mistakes. Not the product, not the price, but service.

You'll lose clients when...you promise to call (e-mail, fax) the client back tomorrow with information and then get really busy (or serve a "more important" client) and forget to do it for a couple of days.

You have now lost credibility and integrity.

You'll lose clients when...estimates, proposals or invoices have errors or don't go out on time.

You have now lost trust and confidence in your ability.

You'll lose clients when...their calls are unanswered and they can't leave a message because your voice mailbox is full. With no set plan for checking the machine, calls get missed and/or returned late, or even worse, not at all. You have now lost the clients sense of importance.

This is what the client now thinks. "Now that I am a client they take me for granted. I can't trust this person to do what they said they would do. If they are not keeping their word on these simple things, how will they treat me on bigger projects? I am not going to buy more products or continue with service if this is how my business will be treated. Is there someone else who can do this for me that is more reliable? I am not going to recommend them and risk my reputation."

Now, I completely understand about making the most of a tight economy and if you have a business where your team members wear multiple hats **and it works,** great.

However all to often I've worked with clients and seen confidence in the company dwindle due to the leader's lack of delegation and attention to details. Put your ego aside and make investments in employees that will help grow and retain your clients. If you have a full team, make sure they are supporting your sales effort. A superstar salesperson can only do so much alone. They can bring in the client and close the sale, but reception, accounting, customer service and manufacturing all need to be just as client centric as the sales department.

Having the best product, service, or price are wonderful attributes. However, I've seen clients pay a little more, or sacrifice a bit in quality and move their business because another company demonstrated a greater commitment to their customer. The money spent on having key people in service jobs will pay for itself when clients trust the company, not just the product or service you provide.

Sales Geisha

Part 4

Recruitment and Retention

Sales Geisha

Shortage of Available Candidates

As the economy grows and companies increase sales positions, recruiting becomes one of the toughest challenges for business leaders. No longer can you post a help wanted ad and have talented reps show up at your door. College-educated sales professionals with several years experience are in high demand, and most of those reps are already working. Businesses of all sizes are fighting for those that are available. Why is it so difficult to find and hire good sales people?

Underlying Causes:
1. Fresh graduates are less likely to join the sales profession. Lackluster classes in sales and marketing, combined with negative stereotypes of salespeople are turning new graduates away from this profession.
2. Unhealthy sales environment. With the high expectations and stresses of many sales jobs, junior salespeople drop out and change careers.
3. Poor training and sales culture, and a lack of career advancement, has allowed for less than desirable sales professionals in the market.
4. Good salespeople are employed and difficult to headhunt. Managers take care of top performers and top performers are hesitant to leave their client portfolio (and income).

How to Find Talent:
1. Review the recruiting budget and be prepared to pay more to find top sales performers.
2. Consider utilizing recruiting sources to reach as many qualified candidates as possible.
3. Protect what you already have! When resources are tight competitors will offer your staff more money, better benefits and opportunity. Don't get poached!
4. Design a recruiting and retention plan. Protect yourself from the high cost of sales attrition.

In order to maximize opportunities you need a top-notch team ready to sell. Build your pipeline now in order to maximize growth.

How to Hire A Top Performer

Want to hire the rainmaker that will change the course of your business? Increase your bottom line by hiring the right sales rep, the first time, by following these five steps.

Know what you are looking for.
Drill down and define the skill set you need on your team. Hire based on the selling role and work environment.

Look in the right places.
Top performing sales reps are usually employed. Don't hire the friend of your neighbor because she's a real "people person." Target specific companies and networks.

Have an Objective Way to Measure Candidates
Determine the hard and soft skills that are important to evaluate, and stick to the plan. Interview, role-play and use behavioral and competency tests.

Measure All Candidates Equally
Use the same standards of assessment for all candidates. Using a base question and answer format prevents the haloing of applicants. Develop scoring criteria to evaluate applicants.

Don't Settle!
Dump the philosophy that a warm body is better than nothing. It's much easier to expand your sales base with the right team than it is to clean the mess up after a poor rep.

How "A" Players Interview

We all want the best talent. But how can we identify the "A" players versus "a player"? The former will make you money, the latter will cost you.

As a sales manager you need to determine if the person sitting across from you in an interview will be an "A" player. Will he or she be the next top producer? Will quota be met? How do you identify your rainmaker in an interview?

An "A" player will be confident. They will proudly brandish accomplishments on their resume. "A" players know their numbers and aren't afraid to talk about them. They can tell you their quotas, their income and their sales plan. He or she will also be able to tell stories of how they closed deals and how they turned tough customers into long-term clients.

Since they know their numbers so well, they will also know their worth. Don't pinch pennies with this one. Competition for top salespeople is tough and the investment is worth the return.

Admitting to your limitations is not easy to do, but "A" players can do it and will happily tell you the truth. They know their strengths and weaknesses, and will tell you what you need to know, not what they think you want to hear.

In an interview this person will ask many questions. Be prepared for a top performer to ask a lot of questions about the job, the future of the job, and the company.

A true "A" player is an expert in his field and has perfected the craft. His experience has armed him with an abundance of best practices, and ways to sell better, faster and more efficiently. Look for this sales gem at your next interview. Give him the job, the goal, and then get out of the way.

Hiring Criteria

You've heard it before; when hiring a salesperson make sure you have a clear description of your sales needs and a detailed screening process. The challenge arises when what you know and what you do, are often two different things. Defining mandatory, versus non-mandatory criteria, allows you to find the best sales fit without wasting time and money on non-qualified candidates.

Required employment categories that you may have for job applicants include: education, years of experience, sales training, communication skills, and proficiency with digital technology. Often it's difficult to find an applicant that is a perfect match for your job description. Decide which criteria are mandatory (must have) and which are non-mandatory (desirable).

Examine the sales lineup you have in place and review what skills are most critical, and what you can live without. Every sales environment is different and a mandatory attribute in pharmaceutical sales may only be a desirable attribute in the technology field. Look back to the most successful reps you employed and dissect their talents and personalities to find common traits, talents and experience. These common factors are what are necessary for the position; the other qualities would be "nice to have."

Also review where there are "holes" in your sales team and use the criteria to balance out the talent. Do you have many educated, mature reps that could use some sales tech help? Make digital technology mandatory. Have lots of tech-heads and need some more formally educated leaders? Make a Graduate Degree mandatory.

Rank your "must-have" and "desirable" attributes. Be mindful when creating the list, as too many filters will result in a restricted pool of candidates. Too few requirements will increase the pool, but can leave you with a load of bad matches. Refer to this list when reviewing resumes and during interviews. This will make the selection process easier. A candidate with all "desirable" factors will not make the cut compared to the applicant with a list of "must-have" attributes.

Create a filter and use it. The filter will increase your hiring success, and you won't waste money and time interviewing less desirable applicants. Identifying what you want (and need) for your team will speed up the hiring process and help you find the perfect candidate.

Avoid the Halo Effect In Sales Hiring

It's easy to like someone based on good looks and personality. A professional with impressive credentials may seem like a great hire. But, does either of these single qualities translate into an exceptional sales person? What really is in play is the "halo effect"; the belief that one good trait means that all traits are equally as good.

Research shows that a high percentage of hires are made based on looks. Fortunately the halo effect becomes less problematic with awareness.   A successful sales manager must work against this bias to evaluate the candidate's actual ability to perform.

Forget about your "gut" feeling and "hunches" in regard to hiring a sales rep. The validity and success of the interviewing process increases when you use a formalized, standardized, objective way of evaluation.

Counterintuitive Recruitment Options

When selecting a sales person for your team, consider options that may seem counterintuitive.

Introvert vs. Extrovert
The best salespeople are outgoing, right? Not necessarily. The stereotype of a backslapping extroverted rep is as outdated as the sales techniques those people used. Introverts often exude composure, self-control, and the ability to build long-term relationships. When hiring, don't automatically choose an extrovert. Your customer may prefer to have a peer rather than a pusher.

Big Company, Big Results?
Hiring someone with experience at a large company will translate into large sales for your second tier company. True? A rep with big league experience may choke selling at a lower profile firm. Find a rep that is the best fit for your sales environment, not the rep that comes with name brand exposure.

Wanting to Be Wanted
Passion for your business is good, but hiring someone based on the love for your product could be a mistake. Don't confuse desire with results. Just because someone wants to work for you, or is willing to accept a low salary, doesn't mean they will be top producers.

Live Tests in The Interview Process

Does your interview process include a mock sales presentation or involve role-playing with the candidate? If presented properly, live tests can demonstrate the sales capabilities of your applicant.

In order for this method to be effective you need to provide presentation guidelines. Asking the job seeker to make a sales pitch without any direction will be frustrating for everyone involved. Instead, explain the process in detail and give your candidate time to prepare prior to the interview. Communicate if this presentation is a cold- call, response to inquiry, or referral. It is best to have your candidate select a topic that enables him to demonstrate industry knowledge and confidence, not necessarily your product. As part of the selection process, have the candidate deliver a 15-minute mock sales pitch to members of the recruitment team. The recruiters will play the role of prospective customers and will evaluate the overall presentation.

In this setting you can assess many sales skills. Evaluate how rapport is built and if the "customers" are engaged. Is the presenter confident or arrogant? Did your candidate display adequate product knowledge, and was the pitch organized and presented in a succinct manner? Was the customer educated about the merchandise or service? When presented with objections, were they overcome easily and comfortably, or did the applicant become agitated and frustrated? Was the image of the company conveyed in the appearance of the presenter? When sidelined by the customer did your applicant react appropriately? Was he able to think on his feet to maintain the sale? Did your "customers" buy?

In addition to sales role-playing you can also request that your candidate prepare a territory plan for you. Ask how sales goals will be met and what customers should be put on a hot list. You may look like you're hunting for leads if you demand a three-month sales plan right out of the gate. However, if a top salesperson is interested in a job, they have already been thinking about opportunities they could seize if given the chance. If your candidate is not excited about selling for you now, they will probably be less enthusiastic (and less productive) later.

An effective interview is more than just a question and answer process. The best interviews will also include live tests, allowing the recruiter to judge the level of preparation, professionalism and organization of the candidate.

Building a Winning Sales Team

Have you ever worked with someone who believed in the principle "If you throw enough mud at a wall, some of it will stick?" This manager will hire, hire, *and* hire, with the belief that one salesperson will eventually be successful. Throw lots of mud, find lots of winners…. eventually. This may sound like a heck of a way to develop your sales staff, but it's not uncommon. Let's throw that technique out the window, and build a team where everyone is successful at the outset.

In order to assemble a great team, first know about your sales. How are you doing today? What are your sales goals and the overall goals of the company? Do you embrace modern selling techniques or are you still holding on to outdated models? What type of salesperson is successful in your company? Before you invest in the recruitment and hiring of new salespeople, have the answers to these questions. Update old practices and procedures and allow for the new hires and yourself to succeed.

With a sales model in place, you can focus on team members. When deciding who to hire, consider who will fit the company culture, rather than looking exclusively for certain skills. Now this doesn't mean go and hire some one you find likeable. It means, that in addition to skills and experience, you need to consider behaviors, personality assessments, and conduct multiple interviews with different managers to get a broad perspective on fit.

Once you've chosen the best players for your team, you need to support them with an onboarding plan. Onboarding is a comprehensive approach to ramping up new hires that exceeds the traditional first day orientation. It makes new salespeople familiar with the overall goals of the company, and supports their work, in an effort to achieve quick success and productivity. Increase sales and reduce turnover by creating, and diligently using, a great onboarding plan.

Sales people aren't just revenue generators; they are also your client-facing representation, the people with the most daily contact with your customers. With that in mind realize it's not only important to build your winning team, but to do it properly.

Hiring A Start-Up Sales Rep

Sales people always face objections. Selling for a start up means facing objections *and* a tremendous amount of resistance. The customer is unfamiliar with the business and has no reason to trust you. You have few (if any) references, no proven merchandise, reputation, or extended track record. The product is usually more expensive and buyers perceive working with you as a risk. In the beginning the founder tackles this sales challenge. As the company grows and develops so does the sales department.

Very few early stage companies are started by salespeople, which means very few early stage founders understand sales. Start up sales is evangelical sales. Your reps need to educate the customer about something new and different, and convince them there is a need for the product. Your seller needs to be able to have your clients take a leap of faith.

This specialized selling requires a specialized rep. Your sales recruiting process must be top notch, should include the use of sales candidate assessments and interview scripts. Startups can't afford to waste money or make hiring mistakes. Top sales producers from brand name employers are often romanced for the job. The thought is that experienced sales reps will bring in sales quickly and easily. That decision is often costly. Superstars from marquee employees don't encounter the type of resistance that start-ups face. In this environment they will fail. They are accustomed to selling mature products with strong reputations. When you have market share and a proven product, look for your superstar. To get it all started you need a maverick.

The maverick is a breed of salesperson that views challenges as opportunities. They function with little internal help and support. They aren't sensitive to risk and they can inspire customers. They are fearless! He will expand your pipeline of leads, handle customer relations and create his own sales proposals while the founder focuses on building the product and running the company.

When hiring a maverick, sell the journey, but don't pretend it will be easy. It won't. Finding someone who has already succeeded with an early stage company increases your chance for success. Get the whole team involved with the hiring, because you will all be working closely together.

Startup sales people are evangelists, hustlers and relationship builders all in one.

Find them and don't let them get away.

Avoid Sales Breakups

There are many reasons sales people fail. They fail to prospect, they fail to overcome objections, to ask for the order, to create a sales plan, or connect with buyers. The list is endless.

It's easy to blame a departing rep for poor performance and make excuses for high turnover in the sales department. But is it really the rep's fault? If you didn't hire properly, offer structured training, and provide a successful environment, the failure is because of you. That's right. Like George Costanza in the comedy Seinfeld, be prepared to say goodbye to your rep by saying, "it's not you, it's me."

What you can do to avoid the "break-up".

Hire Properly. Don't employ someone just because they happen to land on your doorstep. Seek out the best candidates and make sure that person has succeeded in a similar sales environment. Analyze their capabilities and crosscheck references. If you'd like your new hire to become productive quickly, invest in an onboarding program.

Onboarding is a comprehensive approach to ramping up new hires that exceeds the traditional first day orientation. It makes new salespeople familiar with the overall goals of the company, and supports their work in an effort to achieve quick success and productivity. Onboarding may be the last step in recruitment, but it is the first step in retention.

Offer Structured Training. Provide guidance and a formal training plan, including specific training requirements and goals. Every rep should know about the product or service they sell, but that's just the beginning. They need to understand their sales market, as well as their target prospect. Basic selling skills like overcoming objections, new business development, price integrity and customer service should be taught. Offer training and support on a regular basis to ensure success.

Create a Motivating Compensation Package. Base salary, commissions, and sales incentives make up the bulk of a typical salesperson's compensation package. A well-designed program focuses sales energy on activities that support the company's business objectives, and in turn, reward those salespeople for their contributions. The best salaries and incentives create a positive buzz and help the rep and business succeed. Plan on paying out! You want your rep to be a money making machine. If your rep is making money, so are you!

Become the Coach and Define Expectations. Managers have many demands on their time, but even top sellers need a coach. Be part of a positive coaching culture. Help your players by defining clear expectations, and explain how they will be accountable if they don't perform. Show them how to make it happen, then monitor and assess their performance. Establish a formal coaching program, offer advice and measure progress weekly. Provide regular feedback and demonstrate an exciting vision. Rally the team!

Get Out of the Way. Clear away the administration that gets in the way of making sales. Don't slow the reps down with useless paperwork or senseless meetings. Salespeople are judged by the amount of revenue they bring to the establishment. For this reason it is in everyone's best interest to keep the salespeople selling! Don't allow them to waste time on activities that don't add to the bottom line.

Sales people aren't just money-makers; they are also your client-facing representation, the people with the most daily contact with your customers. When you embrace the above structure, you'll discover that sales churn will decrease and profits will increase. Create a culture of success and you'll be left with a profitable, happy, long-term sales relationship.

Sales Geisha

Part 5

Sales Compensation

An Effective Sales Compensation Plan

One of the biggest questions from managers is how to best compensate salespeople. Pay them too little and they will leave. Pay them too much and they'll get lazy. Straight commission is good, no wait, straight commission is bad. You know there is a need for an incentive plan to motivate your team. The problem is that you don't know what it looks like.

Your sales compensation plan has a huge effect on the bottom line. Set up correctly it can yield great results for all. The best salaries and incentives create a positive buzz and your ability to attract talent will increase. Top performers will hang around. No worries about poaching when the money is rolling in.

Base salary, commissions, and sales incentives make up the bulk of a typical salesperson's compensation package. A well-designed program focuses salespeople on activities that support the company's business objectives, and in turn, reward those salespeople for their contributions. New account development is important and so is growing the current client base. What's the formula? What's the right balance between salary and commission? How do you measure success for special incentives? What are you willing to pay to acquire sales growth?

Write the Plan
Connect sales with business goals. Make sure the sales plan is in alignment with the business plan. Are you looking to increase new accounts or sell-in a new product? Design incentive and rewards that drive sales to support your mission.

Simplicity = Success. Keep the plan simple so reps can work effectively and know where to push. A complicated plan that pays out later rather than sooner, or one that is difficult to understand can backfire and de-motivate your team.

Create the perfect recipe. The best plans have the following ingredients- base salary, variable for performance (commission) and incentives tied to specific targets.

Structure. What's the best mix? Evaluate the sales person and what is being sold. The role of the salesperson, the sales cycle, and the kind of selling all factor into the equation of salary vs. commission.

Performance Measures. Guide salespeople in their focus by clearly defining benchmarks and goals. Make sure the target is attainable and results are easily measured.

You want your reps to be big earners. If they make money, you are making more. Feed them, support them, and offer opportunity. Encourage them to work harder and reward them generously.

Sales Compensation Plan Issues

You've developed a solid compensation plan for your reps, yet there are still issues that need to be ironed out. Addressing these topics from the outset will ensure happier salespeople and no problems when it's time to cut the checks.

Reasonable Quotas

Setting quota can be like gambling. If quotas are set too low, the company pays out money it doesn't really have. If quota is too high, reps can get frustrated and leave. What's a fair quota for your reps? Analyze the experience of the seller, the market, and their potential. Keep in mind that a salesperson needs to believe that although their sales goal is difficult, it IS achievable. Set a goal that's fair for the company, yet compliments the individual. If you set quota at a level that's profitable for the company, it won't matter that you're paying reps more money, you'll be happy to do it.

Paying for Repeat Business and Renewals

Repeat business equals more profit, and we know that it costs more to generate new business than it does to sell to an existing customer. Over the last few years the business climate has changed, and some organizations have reduced or eliminated the pay for repeat business, hoping to increase the bottom line. The question posed is, should reps be paid for repeat business and renewals, and if so, should the commission be the same as a new business sale? Consider what is most valuable to you, e.g., new customers, profitable customers, or highest potential customers. The extent to which you need to pay for repeat business and renewals, depends on the degree to which the current plan supports your new business goals and sales strategies.

How to Pay for Bluebirds

Now we're not talking about selling a large bunch of feathered friends, we're talking about pay for an unexpected, very profitable, or easily made sale. If a deal "flies" in and lands in the lap of your rep, do they get the same commission? If your top rep is making a rock star salary based on luck vs. work, it may be time to restructure his pay plan. If you have a hard working rep that occasionally catches a Bluebird, pay the same. That occasional gift can keep a rep motivated during tough times.

Rewarding for Customer Satisfaction

Organizations with higher than average levels of customer satisfaction experience higher profits, higher sales, and higher customer loyalty levels. Differentiate yourself from your competitors by offering a bonus to your reps for high customer rep scores. You'll keep your salespeople, and your clients happy.

Paying for Profit vs. Revenues

Should you pay salespeople based on the amount of profit that the sale produces – or should you pay based on the amount of revenue that is generated? What is your objective for sales this year? Is it to generate revenue (market share) or profit? Match the goals of the company with the compensation plan for the best results. However, if you plan to pay on profit, make sure the profit ratio is clearly defined. Salespeople will walk away from deals (and jobs) if they think there isn't enough profit for them to make commissions.

Keep the compensation plan simple and incentivize multiple behaviors. Pay too much or too little to reach your goals, and you'll hinder your ability to keep your reps, and close the deals.

Sales Compensation Strategies

Changes in the economy have resulted in many businesses reviewing compensation expenses. The sales commission budget – traditionally the largest cost- is often under scrutiny. Can that expense be lowered with a new incentive calculation process? Data shows that 75% of organizations with 1,000-2,500 employees currently determine commissions using spreadsheets. This approach can lead to overpayments on bonuses and commissions, increased risk of error, loss of time, and inaccurate readings of data.

This often complicated procedure can be simpler and more exact with the use of Incentive Compensation Management (ICM). ICM simplifies compensation management while offering a wealth of information.

Loading data into a spreadsheet is time consuming and allows for a high margin of error. When the spreadsheet is complete, you are left with a commission amount and not much else. Incentive Compensation Management delivers accurate payment facts, as well as direct correlations between compensation and performance. You have the flexibility to change the plan duration (monthly, quarterly, annually, etc.), re-calculate commissions with new parameters, and have multiple quotas or multiple forecasts. The most current figures from sales, finance and HR are included without the manual collection of records or modification of formulas. Data is obtained automatically combining the information quickly and accurately.

Yes, there is an expense with an ICM, but with proper use you will almost immediately experience cost savings. Since you are no longer working with complicated spreadsheets, compensation plans can be modified easily and correctly. With access to sales performance versus commission paid, you can monitor sales trends, quota performance, and attainment distributions using real-time dashboards and reporting.

Current incentives are easily visible and sales teams are able to determine their actual and projected commissions. Questions regarding the payout can be done through Incentive Compensation Management and communications are directed to the appropriate parties. All inquires and responses are also traceable, allowing for transparency with the process.

At a time when organizational efficiency and effectiveness are of great importance, Incentive Compensation Management establishes payroll as a seamless business process. A decrease in errors combined with an increase in productivity promise that ICM offers the highest financial return in the shortest amount of time. Limited effort will be spent researching and resolving sales disputes, and with precise sales incentive calculation your team will exert less energy checking on their pay, and more time selling!

Sales Compensation and the Economy

The model of supply and demand is the backbone of price determination in a free market. Demand refers to the amount of product or service that is desired from buyers. Supply represents the amount of products or services provided. The ensuing philosophy dictates that price is a reflection of supply and demand. When there is a large amount of candidates and low supply of jobs, it would make sense to believe that the price (salary) would be reduced as well.

An example: Your favorite band is having a special concert. Because there is a surplus of concerts, the supply and demand market has determined the acceptable ticket price among buyers is forty dollars. So you plan on paying forty dollars for your ticket. In the job market, the same theory looks like this: When employers are hurting financially and receiving hundreds of applicants for a single open position, hiring managers can offer lower salaries for available jobs. You believe you can offer a lower salary too. It's a buyer's market for talent, right? Let's take a closer look.

You go to buy a forty-dollar ticket to the concert and you can't find one. While forty is the standard price for most shows, this is an exclusive performance with limited seats, so these tickets are one hundred fifty dollars. With only a limited supply available, and demand high, the longer you wait for tickets the more expensive they will get, if you can get one at all. Demand has increased for the tickets and so has the price. Your choice is to pay less for a lesser show, or pay more and invest in the top performance you desire.

Hiring the best sales talent is like buying a ticket for the concert. Overall, there are plenty of salespeople to employ, just like there are many concert tickets available to purchase. However, you don't want "any ticket" or "any salesperson," you want the special one, the best. Twenty percent of all salespeople make eighty percent of all sales.

Want cheap? Bargain hunt low performers, and get yourself a down-market deal. Want gold? Dig for the top twenty percent and pay what it takes.

Don't be fooled by the economy. If the market drops, the desire to hire talented sales performers will still increase. In sales recruitment, demand is always high and supply is low. If you think you can offer a lower salary, be prepared for lower sales.

Sales Geisha

ABOUT THE AUTHOR
CHRISTINE MILLER

As the owner of Miller Sales Consulting, Christine helps small businesses identify, develop, and close targeted sales leads, while finding more value in existing client relationships through sales and marketing solutions. The scope of her experience has spanned virtually all aspects of sales and marketing, with a focus in business development, sales training and sales management.

www.ingramcontent.com/pod-product-compliance
Lightning Source LLC
Chambersburg PA
CBHW040836180526
45159CB00001B/206